FOR MY MUSICAL
SISTER-IN-LAW

WITH CHRISTMAS
LOVE -
HEATHER

25.12.11

Richard Baker's
CLASSICAL MUSIC QUIZ BOOK

Over 600 Questions

Richard Baker's

CLASSICAL
MUSIC
QUIZ
BOOK

from Bach *to* Bernstein

OMNIBUS PRESS

London/New York/Paris/Sydney/Copenhagen/Berlin/Madrid/Tokyo

Published by
Omnibus Press
a division of Music Sales Limited
14 -15 Berners Street, London W1T 3L J, UK.

Exclusive Distributors:
Music Sales Limited
Distribution Centre, Newmarket Road, Bury St Edmunds, Suffolk IP33 3YB, UK.
Music Sales Corporation
257 Park Avenue South, New York, NY 10010, United States of America.
Music Sales Pty Limited
120 Rothschild Avenue, Rosebery, NSW 2018, Australia.

This book © Copyright 2006 Wise Publications
a division of Music Sales Limited.

Order No: AM985347
ISBN 1-84609-503-4

Project editor: Ann Farmer
Cover and book design by Chloë Alexander

Your Guarantee of Quality
As publishers, we strive to produce every book to the highest commercial standards.
Throughout, the printing and binding have been planned to ensure a sturdy, attractive
publication which should give years of enjoyment.
If your copy fails to meet our high standards, please inform us and we will gladly replace it.

www.musicsales.com

Contents

Foreword

IF YOU ARE OF MY GENERATION, OR ANYTHING LIKE IT, you may remember the entertaining quiz *Face the Music* on BBC2. It ran on and off for some 14 years in the late sixties and through the seventies.

Joseph Cooper was the genial host. He presided at the pianoforte, upon which he played his brilliantly ingenious 'Hidden Melodies' to tease the wits of his victims. I was frequently one of them, along with Joyce Grenfell and Robin Ray, David Attenborough, Bernard Levin, Patrick Moore and others. It didn't really matter if you got the answer wrong. There were only three panellists in each programme—there was no competing team in the studio. But competition often did come from the unseen audience at home who would sometimes write reproach to take us to task for some particularly stupid lapse. I got things wrong as often as anyone and since then I've found it safer to be the one who sets the questions in a music quiz.

During the last 20 years I have been in that position many many times in the course of the Music Festivals at Sea which I have hosted for P&O cruises, and in this book I have put together more than 600 questions that I have tried out on P&O passengers. It is always a surprise to discover what people do and don't know. What you think is a tough question sometimes causes no trouble at all, whereas what you think is easy leaves everyone totally stumped.

The questions you will find here cover a wide variety of musical topics and varying degrees of difficulty. I hope you will find them interesting, whether you know the answers or not, and that they will provide you with ammunition if you feel like organising a quiz among your family and friends. At the end you will find some tie-breakers, in case your victims notch up the same score. Here the nearest guess wins.

I must record my debt to Michael Kennedy, whose *Oxford Dictionary Of Music* has been my most useful source of information, and who invented—for a P&O music quiz—most of the musical anagrams you will find here.

Have fun!

Richard Baker

Composers & Conductors

1 Who was appointed conductor of the Philadelphia Orchestra in 1912 and retained the post until 1937?

2 Which famous 19th-century composer was the son of a village butcher?

3 Towards the end of the 19th century there was an important group of five Russian composers known as 'the mighty handful'. Four of them were Balakirev, Borodin, Moussorgsky and César Cui. Who was the fifth?

4 Who was the first permanent conductor of the BBC Symphony Orchestra?

5 How old was Mendelssohn when he composed the overture to *A Midsummer Night's Dream*?

6 Which member of the Strauss family was a talented architect and engineer who invented a street-cleaning machine for the city of Vienna and had to be coerced into the family music business when his brother fell ill?

Round 1

Composers & Conductors

7 Brahms was a great admirer of Johann Strauss II, and one day when he was asked to autograph a fan belonging to Strauss's wife, he wrote the first notes of a waltz by Strauss on the fan and added the comment underneath: 'Unfortunately not by Johannes Brahms.' What was the waltz?

8 In 1841, the *London Musical World* published the following comment on a leading contemporary musician:

'The entire works of BLANK present a motley surface of ranting hyperbole and excruciating cacophony; but there is an excuse at the moment. He is entrammelled in the enthralling bonds of that arch-enchantress Georges Sand, but we wonder how she can be content to wanton away her dream-like existence with an artistic nonentity like BLANK.' Who was *BLANK*?

9 Johann Strauss I had a rival in the same line of business. Each of them had his own orchestra and fashionable Vienna was divided into opposing groups of admirers. Who was the elder Strauss's rival?

10 Which British conductor was known to orchestral players as 'Old Timber'?

11 In 1929 an orchestral arrangement of Bach's ***Toccata And Fugue In D Minor*** was introduced at the Proms. It was attributed to Paul Klenovsky, but who really made the arrangement?

12 Which 19th-century Russian composer was a naval officer as a young man?

13 When Frederick Delius became blind and paralysed, who took down his music from dictation?

14 Which great composer married Constanze Weber?

15 Which Venetian composer was known as 'The Red Priest'?

16 Three famous British composers died in 1934. Who were they?

17 In which city was J.S. Bach cantor of St Thomas's Church?

18 Who was the Irish conductor and composer who was born at Hillsborough Co. Down, wrote an Irish Symphony, and was conductor of the Hallé orchestra 1920–1933?

19 Which 17th-century French musician died after stabbing himself in the foot with the mace he used for conducting?

20 Which Spanish composer died when his ship the S.S. 'Sussex' was torpedoed in the English channel in 1916?

21 A well-known Spanish composer made his debut as a pianist in Barcelona when he was four, and at the age of 12 stowed away in a ship bound from Cadiz to South America. After this he toured the Americas on his own for a year and then returned to settle in Barcelona.
Best known for his suite of 12 piano pieces entitled *Iberia* and for a famous tango. Who was he?

22 Who was the impresario who invited Joseph Haydn to London twice in the 1790s?

Composers & Conductors

23 What was the name of Robert Schumann's wife before he married her?

24 Which composer's imaginary Toccata is the subject of a poem by Robert Browning?

25 Who was the conductor of the Concertgebouw Orchestra in Amsterdam from 1895–1941 and made it world-famous?

26 Which leading 19th-century Russian composer was also a professor of chemistry?

27 Who composed *Hamlet—a Fantasy Overture after Shakespeare*?

28 Which great composer is said to have walked 200 miles as a young man from Arnstadt to Lübeck to hear Dietrich Buxtehude play the organ?

29 Which two London orchestras were founded by Sir Thomas Beecham?

30 Between 1837 and 1839 a well-known musician was musical director at the opera house in Riga, now the capital of Latvia. He got into debt and to escape his creditors decided to go to London. With that intention he boarded the schooner 'Thetis' with his wife and Newfoundland dog, Robber. The journey, which should have taken eight days, in fact lasted three-and-a-half weeks because the 'Thetis' encountered terrible storms in the Skagerrak and had to take refuge in the Norwegian village of Sandvika. This experience proved a source of operatic inspiration to the musician in question. Who was he?

31 Which English composer was imprisoned in Holloway jail for her support of the suffragette movement and wrote the movement's anthem *The March of the Women*?

32 Sir William Walton made his home on which Mediterranean island?

33 Which German composer wrote an opera and a symphony inspired by the medieval painter Matthias Grünewald?

34 Who was appointed cantor of St Thomas's church, Leipzig, in preference to J.S. Bach, but decided to remain in Hamburg when that city made him a better offer?

35 Which composer is alleged to have poisoned Mozart?

36 In which town was Sir Malcolm Sargent born?

37 Which British composer went with Sir George Grove in 1867 to Vienna to search for lost Schubert scores and found the missing movements of the *Rosamunde* music?

38 Who was the Russian composer born in 1872 who had strange mystical ideas and wrote *Poem of Ecstasy* and *Prometheus, Poem of Fire*?

39 Which composer worked as an orange grower in Florida as a young man and wrote a *Florida Suite*?

40 Who called the relatively slight compositions of his later years *Sins Of My Old Age*?

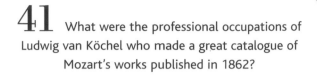

41 What were the professional occupations of Ludwig van Köchel who made a great catalogue of Mozart's works published in 1862?

42 Who said to Mozart's father when he was on a visit to Vienna: 'Before God and as an honest man, I tell you that your son is the greatest composer known to me either in person or by name'?

43 Under what pseudonym did Philip Heseltine compose?

44 Grieg had a house built for himself near Bergen. What is it called?

45 Who conducted the first performance in 1839 of Schubert's 'Great' Symphony In C Major?

46 Whose autobiography is called *A Mingled Chime*?

47 Who became conductor of the Philadelphia Orchestra in 1938?

48
Who succeeded Toscanini as conductor of the New York Philharmonic in 1936?

49
In 1920, a music critic dubbed half-a-dozen young avant-garde French composers 'Les Six'. Five of them were Georges Auric, Louis Durey, Arthur Honegger, Darius Milhaud and Germaine Tailleferre. Who was the sixth?

50
What was the name of the beloved sister with whom Mendelssohn played piano duets as a child and who died a few months before Mendelssohn himself in 1847?

51
What's the name of the Indian musician born in Mumbai (Bombay) in 1936 who won first prize in the Liverpool International Conductors Competition in 1958 and went on to become one of the world's leading conductors?

52
On one occasion when a friend was visiting Beethoven, the composer pointed to the works of a certain earlier musician on his shelves and said: 'There lies the Truth.' Whose works was he referring to?

53 Which famous composer and pianist visited by Edvard Grieg in Rome played through Grieg's piano concerto at sight, orchestral parts and all?

54 By what name is Mahler's protégé Bruno Schlesinger better known?

55 Who was the wealthy widow who made Tchaikovsky an annual allowance for over a decade though they never met?

56 A well-known musician wrote to a friend from a Mediterranean island in the winter of 1838: 'I caught a bad cold. The three most celebrated doctors in the island met for a consultation. The first said that I would die. The second that I was dying. The third that I was already dead. Thank God I am now myself again. But my illness interfered with my preludes.'
Who was the musician?

57 What was the real name of Chopin's friend Georges Sand?

Composers & Conductors

1 Leopold Stokowski (1882–1977)

2 Antonin Dvořák (1841–1904)

3 Nikolay Andreyevich Rimsky-Korsakov (1844–1908)

4 Sir Adrian Boult (1889–1983)

5 Seventeen

6 Josef Strauss (1827–1870)

7 The Blue Danube

8 Frédéric Chopin (1810–1849)

9 Josef Lanner (1801–1843)

10 Sir Henry Wood (1869–1944)

11 Sir Henry Wood. 'Klen' is the Russian word for a maple tree.

12 Nikolay Andreyevich Rimsky-Korsakov

13 Eric Fenby (1906–1997)

14 Wolfgang Amadeus Mozart (1756–1791)

15 Antonio Vivaldi (1678–1741)

16 Elgar, Delius, Holst

17 Leipzig

18 Sir Hamilton Harty (1879–1941)

19 Jean-Baptiste Lully (1632–1687)

20 Enrique Granados (1867–1916)

21 Isaac Albéniz (1860–1909)

22 Johann Peter Salomon (1745–1815)

23 Clara Wieck (1819–1896)

24 Baldassare Galuppi (1706–1785). 'A Toccata of Galuppi's'.

25 Willem Mengelberg (1871–1951)

26 Alexander Borodin (1833–1887)

27 Pyotr Tchaikovsky (1840–1893)

28 Johann Sebastian Bach (1685–1750)

29 The London Philharmonic (1932) and the Royal Philharmonic (1946).

30 Richard Wagner (1813–1883). The voyage helped to inspire *The Flying Dutchman*.

31 Dame Ethel Smyth (1858–1944)

32 Ischia

33 Paul Hindemith (1895–1963) The opera *Mathis der Maler* was premiered in Zürich 1938; the symphony *Mathis der Maler* was first performed in Berlin in 1934.

34 Georg Philipp Telemann (1681–1767)

35 Antonio Salieri (1750–1825)

36 Ashford, Kent. The family home was Stamford, Lincs, but Mrs Sargent was staying with a friend, Amy Watts. Baby Malcolm was christened Harold Malcolm Watts Sargent.

37 Sir Arthur Sullivan (1842–1900)

38 Alexander Scriabin (1872–1915)

39 Frederick Delius (1862–1934)

40 Gioachino Rossini (1792–1868)

41 Botany and Mineralogy

42 Joseph Haydn (1732–1809)

43 Peter Warlock (1894–1930)

44 Troldhaugen

45 Felix Mendelssohn (1809–1847)

46 Sir Thomas Beecham (1879–1961)

47 Eugene Ormandy (1899–1985)

48 Sir John Barbirolli (1899–1970)

49 Francis Poulenc (1899–1963)

50 Fanny Mendelssohn (1805–1847)

51 Zubin Mehta (1936–)

52 George Frideric Handel (1685–1759)

53 Franz Liszt (1811–1886)

54 Bruno Walter (1876–1962)

55 Nadezhda von Meck (1831–1894)

56 Frédéric Chopin

57 She was born Amandine Lucile Aurore Dupin. Her married name was Baroness Dudevant.

Songs & Singers

1 In 1908, the song *I Hear You Calling Me* was offered to a 24-year-old singer whose recording of it became the best-selling acoustic record ever made, achieving sales of 4,150,000 copies. Who was the singer?

2 Which Irish composer made a setting of Tennyson's lines which begin 'Come into the garden, Maud'?

3 Sullivan's *The Lost Chord* (1877) was a great commercial success, notching up sales of half a million copies in 25 years. The Prince of Wales declared he would travel the length of his kingdom to hear it sung by Sullivan's close friend Mrs Fanny Ronalds. It was written as a memorial to whom?

4 *Roses of Picardy*, published in 1916, was one of the most beloved songs of World War I.
It had words by Fred E. Weatherly. The composer was born into a musical family in Yorkshire and given as a first name the surname of a famous 18th-century musician.
So who composed *Roses of Picardy*?

5 Which famous soprano was born Helen Mitchell, became Mrs Helen Armstrong and adopted a stage name derived from her native city, which in due course was bestowed on an ice-cream pudding and a kind of toast?

6 Which Australian soprano was born in 1926 in Sydney and became known as 'La Stupenda' thanks to her brilliance in bel canto roles such as Donizetti's *Lucia di Lammermoor*?

7 Who is the New Zealand soprano who was born at Gisborne, Auckland in 1944 and caused a sensation with the hat she wore at the wedding of the Prince of Wales in St Paul's Cathedral in 1981?

8 Who wrote the music to the song *Sea Fever*?

9 Which American singer had a triumph in the role of Joe in Kern's *Showboat* when it came to Drury Lane in London in May 1928?

10 Which popular French cabaret singer was said to be the most famous Corsican since Napoleon?

11 Michael Maybrick composed a great many popular ballads including *The Holy City* using a pseudonym. What was it?

12 Which singer was known as 'The Swedish Nightingale'?

13 Who was the famous Danish, later American, Wagnerian tenor who was born in Copenhagen in 1890 and died in Santa Monica in 1973?

14 Who first recorded (in 1939) *Lili Marlene*?

15 Which popular Neopolitan song, associated with ice-cream cornets, was created in 1898 by Giovanni Capurro and Edoardo de Capua?

16 Which American singer joined the French resistance in the second world war and served in it with distinction? Later she ran a multi-racial orphanage in the Dordogne.

17 Who was the singer and folk-song collector who, in 1905, started collecting songs in the Hebrides and published them in several volumes?

18 What is the name of a type of Portuguese folk song, a bit like Spanish flamenco, which originated in the low dives of Lisbon in the 19th century and is still performed in cafes, cabarets and night clubs in Portugal, often with improvised words?

19 Who was not likely to have a stylish marriage?

20 The real name of a famous singer was Cecilia Sophia Anna Maria Kalogeropoulou. What was her professional name?

21 Which record producer was the husband of Elizabeth Schwarzkopf?

22 Who is the husband of Dame Joan Sutherland?

23 Who composed the Indian Love Lyrics?

24 In 1880 Luigi Denza composed *Funiculi Funicula* to celebrate the building of a funicular railway up which mountain?

25 Which singer made the first classical record to sell one million copies?

26 What is the title of a song by Sir Henry Bishop incorporated in a volume of so-called national airs in 1821, where it is described as Sicilian? To continue the Italian connection, Bishop included it in his 1823 opera *Clari, the Maid of Milan*. In fact it is so well known in this country that we take it for a British national air.

27 Who was the Swedish tenor (born 1911) who sang in a family quartet and became a major star of the New York Met from 1938–59? He died in 1960 at the age of 49.

28 Which British nautical song was quoted by Handel in his *Occasional Oratorio*, by Beethoven in his *Battle Symphony*, was used by Beethoven as a theme for piano variations, formed the subject of an overture by Wagner and was even suggested as the hidden theme of Elgar's *Enigma Variations*?

29 What colour was Jeannie's hair?

30 Which is the nearest figure to the number of songs written by Schubert: 6, 60, 600 or 6,000?

31 Who composed *Night And Day*, *Anything Goes*, *Let's Do It*, and *Brush Up Your Shakespeare*?

32 Which cabaret artist was associated with the song *Darling, Je Vous Aime Beaucoup*?

33 Name the tenor born in Modena in 1935 who appeared at the Llangollen International Eisteddfod as a member of his local choir, partnered Dame Joan Sutherland as Edgardo in *Lucia di Lammermoor* and made a Puccini aria universally famous by singing it to the crowd at the World Cup in 1990?

34 Who composed *Say it with Music*?

35 Which French song written in 1792 was originally called *Chant de Guerre pour l'Armée du Rhin* (War Song for the Rhine Army)?

36 Who wrote *I Got Rhythm, Bidin' My Time* and *Nice Work If You Can Get It*?

37 Who composed *Silent Noon*, *Bright Is The Ring of Words* and *The Roadside Fire*?

38 Who was the Irish poet and musician who between 1807 and 1834 brought out ten sets of 'Irish Melodies', some with his own words and music, some adapted from Irish folk tunes?

39 Hector Grant, Peter Allison, Denton Thomas, Gilbert Miller and J. P. McCall were all pseudonyms for which well-known singer?

40 Which female soprano, born in 1987, released an album entitled *Pure* which included classical, light pop and traditional Maori songs?

1   John McCormack (1884–1945)

2   Michael Balfe (1808–1870)

3   Sullivan's brother Fred (the first Judge in *Trial by Jury*) who died in 1877.

4   Haydn Wood (1882–1959)

5   Dame Nellie Melba (1861–1931)

6   Dame Joan Sutherland (1926–)

7   Dame Kiri te Kanawa (1944–)

8   John Ireland (1879–1962)

9   Paul Robeson (1898–1976)

10   Tino Rossi (1907–1983)

11   Stephen Adams (1844–1913)

12   Jenny Lind (1820–1887)

13   Lauritz Melchior (1890–1973)

14   Lale Andersen (1910–1972). Danish singer. Her *Lili Marlene* was the first German recording to sell a million copies.

15   O Sole Mio

16   Josephine Baker (1906–1975)

17   Marjory Kennedy-Fraser (1857–1930)

18   Fado

19   *Daisy Bell* or *A Bicycle Built For Two*; composed by Harry Dacre in 1892, was one of the most popular music-hall songs on both sides of the Atlantic.

20   Maria Callas (1923–1977)

21   Walter Legge (1906–1979)

Answers

22   Richard Bonynge (1930–)

23   Amy Woodforde-Finden (1860–1919)

24   Vesuvius

25   Enrico Caruso (1873–1921)

26   Home Sweet Home

27   Jussi Björling

28   Rule Britannia

29   Light Brown. *I Dream Of Jeannie With The Light Brown Hair* (song by Stephen Foster).

30   600

31   Cole Porter (1891–1964)

32   Hildegarde (Hildegard Loretta Sell) 1906—she retired aged 89 in 1998.

33   Luciano Pavarotti (1935–)

34   Irving Berlin (Israel Baline 1888–1989)

35   The Marseillaise (so called because it was sung by a battalion of troops from Marseilles as they entered Paris).

36   George Gershwin (1898–1937)

37   Ralph Vaughan Williams (1872–1958)

38   Thomas Moore (1779–1852)

39   Peter Dawson, Australian bass-baritone (1882–1961).

40   Hayley Westenra (1987-)

Words By....

1 Who arranged the text of Handel's *Messiah*?

2 Cole Porter wrote the music for
I Get A Kick Out Of You. Who wrote the words?

3 Sir William Walton wrote the music to *Façade*.
Who wrote the poems?

4 Who wrote the poem *The Dream Of Gerontius*,
set to music by Elgar?

5 *Serenade To Music* by Vaughan Williams is a setting
of lines by whom?

6 Who wrote the words to *Indian Love Lyrics*, with
music by Amy Woodforde-Finden?

7 Who wrote the words to *Land Of Hope And Glory*?

8 The best-known setting of *The Road to Mandalay* is by the American Oley Speaks. Who wrote the poem?

9 Probably the best-known Irish tune is the one generally known as *Londonderry Air*.
Several sets of words have been written for it.
Who wrote the best known lyric for that tune, *Danny Boy*?

10 Who wrote the librettos for Mozart's operas *The Marriage Of Figaro*, *Don Giovanni* and *Così Fan Tutte*?

11 Who wrote the poem of Schubert's song *The Erl King*?

12 Who wrote the words to *Rule Britannia*?

1 Charles Jennens (1700–1773). Noted for his 'wealth, eccentricity and ostentatious style', Jennens thought his contribution to *Messiah* was more important than Handel's, though he admitted that Handel had produced 'a fine entertainment'.

2 Cole Porter (1891–1964), equally at home as composer and wordsmith.

3 Dame Edith Sitwell (1887–1964). It was when the young Walton was living with the Sitwells in the early twenties that *Façade* was conceived.

4 Cardinal John Henry Newman (1801–1890) wrote *The Dream Of Gerontius* in 1866. Elgar started sketching his musical work 30 years later.

5 William Shakespeare (1564–1616). The lines come from *The Merchant Of Venice*.

6 Laurence Hope (nom de plume of Adela Florence Nicholson).

7 A. C. Benson added words to the trio tune of Elgar's *Pomp And Circumstance March No. 1* to form part of Elgar's *Coronation Ode*.

8 Rudyard Kipling (1865–1936). It's often said that some of his geographical details are wrong.

9 Fred E. Weatherley (1848–1929), Somerset lawyer and songwriter who wrote some 1,500 song lyrics.

10 Lorenzo Da Ponte (1739–1838)

11 Johann Wolfgang Goethe (1749–1832). Goethe showed no interest in Schubert's settings of his words.

12 Probably by James Thomson (1700–1748) in 1740.

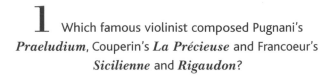

Instruments & Instrumentalists

1 Which famous violinist composed Pugnani's *Praeludium*, Couperin's *La Précieuse* and Francoeur's *Sicilienne* and *Rigaudon*?

2 In 1932 which 16-year-old boy recorded Elgar's violin concerto with the 75-year-old composer conducting?

3 Who is the violinist who, at the age of 16, got 100% in his London Performing Diploma playing Brahms' violin concerto, even though his teacher had threatened to withdraw him from the exam two weeks earlier because he was playing too much jazz?

4 To what note is the bottom string of the 'cello tuned?

5 For how many years was Charles Marie Widor organist at St. Sulpice in Paris?

6 What was the family name of an uncle and nephew who were successively organists at St Mark's Cathedral in Venice between 1566 and 1612?

7 Who was the Norwegian violin virtuoso and enthusiast for Norwegian folk music who was born, like Grieg, in Bergen and had a great influence on Grieg?

8 Which family of instruments is classified as the Aerophones?

9 Which violin virtuoso commissioned Berlioz to write a work for viola and orchestra which resulted in *Harold in Italy*?

10 Who was the great Catalan cellist who went into voluntary exile from Franco's Spain and established a festival in the French Pyrenean village of Prades?

11 Which world-famous conductor played cello in the first performance of Verdi's opera *Otello* in 1887?

12 For which violinist did Brahms write his violin concerto?

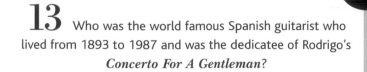

13 Who was the world famous Spanish guitarist who lived from 1893 to 1987 and was the dedicatee of Rodrigo's *Concerto For A Gentleman*?

14 The late Yehudi Menuhin did a lot to encourage interest in Indian music, not least through his concert partnership with Ravi Shankar. Shankar's instrument may be described as a long-necked lute with 18 moveable frets and a number of under-strings to increase resonance. What is it called?

15 Who was the clarinettist and broadcaster who succeeded Reginald Kell as principal in Sir Thomas Beecham's Royal Philharmonic Orchestra and stayed there for 16 years?

16 Which famous organist was born in Alsace in 1875, became an authority on Bach and a medical missionary in Africa?

17 Which figure in antiquity is said to have charmed trees and animals with his lute?

18 For which instrument was Mozart's last concerto written?

19 Who was the player for whom Mozart wrote his clarinet quintet and clarinet concerto?

20 Who was Mozart's horn-playing friend?

21 Which great composer transcribed ten of Vivaldi's violin concertos for harpsichord or organ?

22 What was Sir Malcolm Arnold's instrument when he was an orchestral player?

23 Which English composer of Swedish descent played the trombone on seaside piers as a young man?

24 Lionel Tertis wrote a book called *Cinderella No More* about which orchestral instrument?

25 Which Northern Ireland-born musician is often referred to as 'The Man with the Golden Flute'?

26 What was the name of the Italian keyboard maker and inventor of the piano who was in service to Prince Ferdinando de' Medici from 1690?

27 Which instrument was first produced in Vienna during the 1820s, in imitation of the Chinese sheng?

28 In which work does Czech composer Bedřich Smetana portray the onset of deafness?

1 Fritz Kreisler(1875–1962). Kreisler led critics up the garden path by attributing some of his pieces to 17th- and 18th-century composers but eventually admitted the deception.

2 Yehudi Menuhin (1916–1999)

3 Nigel Kennedy (1956–)

4 c

5 63

6 Gabrieli: Andrea (1510–1586) and Giovanni (1554–1612)

7 Ole Bull (1810–1880)

8 Wind instruments

9 Niccolo Paganini (1782–1840) Paganini never played *Harold in Italy* but gave Berlioz 20,000 francs all the same.

10 Pau (Pablo) Casals (1876–1973)

11 Arturo Toscanini (1867–1957)

12 Joseph Joachim (1831–1907)

13 Andres Segovia (1893–1987). Segovia did a great deal to revive interest in the guitar as a classical instrument. A number of composers wrote works for him.

14 The sitar

15 Jack Brymer (1915–2003)

16 Albert Schweitzer (1875–1965)

17 Orpheus. Whether he really played the lute we don't know, but he does in Shakespeare's song *Orpheus with his Lute*.

18 Clarinet

19 Anton Stadler (1753–1812)

20 Ignaz Leutgeb (c.1745–1811) Mozart wrote four concertos for Leutgeb, who ran a cheese shop in Vienna.

21 Johann Sebastian Bach (1685–1750)

22 Trumpet. At one time principal of the London Philharmonic.

23 Gustav Holst (1874–1934)

24 The Viola. Tertis was the leading British player of that instrument in his generation.

25 James Galway (1939–)

26 Bartolomeo Cristofori (1655–1731)

27 Harmonica

28 The String Quartet No. 1 in E Minor (*From My Life*)

The Musical Theatre: *Opera*

1 Who completed Puccini's opera *Turandot*?

2 A London newspaper reported thus in the year 1900 on a new opera:

'Those who were present were little prepared for the torture and murder scenes taken from Sardou's play. What has music to do with a lustful man chasing a defenceless woman or the dying kicks of a murdered scoundrel.'

Which opera was being described in these terms?

3 What is the name of the opera by Michael Balfe first performed in November 1843 at Drury Lane Theatre where it ran for 100 consecutive performances?

4 There were three operas produced during the Victorian period which became known collectively as *The English Ring*. Two of them were *The Lily Of Killarney* (Benedict) and *Maritana* (Wallace). What was the third?

5 A trio of fruits cause passion in an opera by Prokofiev. Which one?

6 Benjamin Britten wrote a children's opera about the building of Noah's Ark. What is it called?

7 What opera by Wagner is about the phantom captain of a phantom ship?

8 Which opera house in Venice was disastrously burnt in 1996 and has now risen again from the ashes?

9 Which opera by Puccini was first performed on 10 December 1910 at the Metropolitan Opera in New York?

10 The central character of Mozart's opera *Idomeneo* is king of which Greek island?

11 For which institution did Verdi compose *Aïda*?

12 Who wrote an opera called *The Goose Of Cairo*?

13 What is the first of the operas in Wagner's *Ring*?

14 Which opera did Verdi compose for St Petersburg in 1862?

15 Which opera by Verdi was based on the true story of the assassination of a Swedish king (Gustavus III) at a court ball in the year 1792?

16 The Romanian soprano Angela Gheorghiu is married to which operatic tenor?

17 In Gian Carlo Menotti's *The Night Visitors*, who are the visitors?

18 *Cavalleria Rusticana* was composed by Pietro Mascagni. Who wrote the story and play on which it was based?

19 Which opera begins with a servant measuring a floor in a country house near Seville?

20 Which opera by Verdi is about a popular uprising in Palermo (Sicily) in 1282 which led to the end of Angevin rule in that island?

21 Who wrote the play which provided the story of *Madam Butterfly*?

Round 5

22 Which opera by Mozart is set in the country palace of Pasha Selim on the Mediterranean coast of Turkey?

23 The first act of a Wagner opera is set in a Norwegian fishing village. Which opera?

24 In Bizet's opera *The Pearl Fishers*, two fishermen, in what was formerly Ceylon, sing a famous duet of their love for a certain Brahmin priestess. What is her name?

25 In Puccini's *La Bohème* what is the name of the flirtatious girlfriend of the painter Marcello?

26 In which opera do two young men disguise themselves as Albanians and make advances to each other's sweethearts?

27 *The Marriage of Figaro* and *The Barber of Seville* are both based on plays by which French author?

28 Which opera set in India contains the famous *Bell Song* and a duet for two women which provided 'The World's Favourite Airline' with its signature tune?

29 *Ariodante*, *Alcina* and *Atalanta* are all operas by which composer?

30 For which operatic castrato did Mozart write his beloved *Alleluia*?

31 Which character in Puccini's *Turandot* sings the immortal *Nessun Dorma*?

32 Which woman, in an opera named after her, kisses the severed head of the man she loves?

33 Sir William Walton wrote an opera about a son of King Priam of Troy and his lady-love. What are their names?

34 Handel's *Largo* was originally an aria in his opera *Xerxes* addressed to whom or what?

35 Who in 1955 was the first black soloist to appear at the New York Met?

36 Which character comes before the curtain to sing the Prologue to Leoncavallo's opera *Pagliacci*?

37 Who conducted the first complete studio recording of Wagner's *Ring*?

38 Who was the producer of this recording?

39 Which opera subtitled *Wedded Love* was first seen in Vienna in 1805?

40 What was Susanna's secret?

41 How many girls is Don Giovanni (Don Juan) said to have seduced in Spain?

42 Beethoven wrote four overtures for his opera *Fidelio*. One is called 'Fidelio'. What are the other three called?

43 Who composed the opera *Mozart and Salieri*?

44 Did Leoncavallo compose *La Bohème*?

45 What is the name of the birdcatcher in *The Magic Flute*?

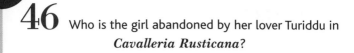

46 Who is the girl abandoned by her lover Turiddu in *Cavalleria Rusticana*?

47 Who wrote the operas *L'Amico Fritz*, *Iris* and *Guglielmo Ratcliff*?

48 In which opera is there a statue which comes to dinner?

49 Which opera by Wagner is set in Rome in the 14th century and concerns a man known as 'the Last of the Tribunes'?

50 What is the name of Madam Butterfly's faithless husband?

51 Which faithful young woman loves an army corporal, brings him news from home and money from his mother's savings, even though he prefers a girl who makes cigarettes?

52 What is the title of Sir Arthur Sullivan's serious opera produced in 1891?

53 Who is the keeper of the harem in Mozart's opera *The Seraglio*?

54 Who is the 'fallen woman' in *La Traviata*?

55 Which opera by Handel has a major role for Cleopatra?

56 Who composed *The Threepenny Opera*?

57 Which opera by Malcolm Williamson based on a novel by Graham Greene was produced in 1963?

58 Which opera by Puccini has an all-female cast?

59 In which opera by Donizetti does Queen Elizabeth I meet Mary Queen of Scots?

60 The Last Rose of Summer was used by the German composer Friedrich von Flotow as the theme tune to an opera set in England in the time of Queen Anne. What is its title?

61 In Mozart's *The Marriage of Figaro*, what's the first name of the Countess Almaviva?

62 In 1850 Franz Liszt conducted the first performance of which opera by Wagner?

1   Franco Alfano (1875–1954)

2   *Tosca* (Puccini)

3   *The Bohemian Girl*

4   *The Bohemian Girl*

5   *The Love for Three Oranges*

6   *Noye's Fludde*

7   *The Flying Dutchman*

8   La Fenice (which appropriately means 'the Phoenix')

9   *La fanciulla del West* ('The Girl of the Golden West')

10   Crete

11   Cairo Opera House

12   Mozart. *L'Oca del Cairo* (1783) is an unfinished two-act comic opera.

13   *Das Rheingold*

14   *La forza del destino* ('The Force of Destiny')

15   *Un ballo in maschera* ('A Masked Ball')

16   Roberto Alagna (1963–)

17   The Magi (the Three Wise Men)

18   Giovanni Verga (1840–1922), a distinguished master of the 'verismo' style.

19   *The Marriage of Figaro*. The valet Figaro is measuring the apartment he plans to share with Susanna once they are married.

20   *Les Vêpres Siciliennes* ('The Sicilian Vespers'), written for Paris Opera.

21   David Belasco (1853–1931)

22   *Die Entführung aus dem Serail* ('The Abduction from the Seraglio'). Often just called 'The Seraglio' in English.

23   *The Flying Dutchman*

24	Leila
25	Musetta
26	*Così fan Tutte* (That's how all women behave)
27	Pierre Beaumarchais (1732–1799)
28	*Lakmé* (Délibes)
29	George Frideric Handel (1685–1759)
30	Venanzio Rauzzini (1746–1810)
31	Prince Calaf
32	*Salome*, in the opera of that name by Richard Strauss. The head is that of John the Baptist.
33	*Troilus and Cressida*
34	A Tree. Xerxes is grateful for the shade it affords from the desert sun.
35	Marian Anderson (1897–1993)
36	Tonio
37	Sir Georg Solti (1912–1997)
38	John Culshaw (1924–1980)
39	Fidelio (Beethoven)
40	She smoked. The one-act *Il segreto di Susanna* was composed by Ermanno Wolf-Ferrari (1876–1948).
41	1,003. In Mozart's *Don Giovanni*, the servant Leporello catalogues his master's conquests in a number of European countries.
42	Leonora Nos.1, 2 and 3
43	Nicolai Rimsky-Korsakov (1844–1908)
44	Yes. Leoncavallo's version was first performed in Venice in 1897. Puccini's was first seen in Turin in 1896.
45	Papageno
46	Santuzza

47   Pietro Mascagni (1863–1945)

48   *Don Giovanni*. The statue of the Commendatore, murdered by Giovanni, comes terrifyingly to life and drags Giovanni off to Hell.

49   *Rienzi*

50   Lieutenant B.F. Pinkerton, USN

51   Micaela (in Bizet's *Carmen*)

52   *Ivanhoe* (based on the novel by Sir Walter Scott)

53   Osmin

54   Violetta Valéry

55   *Julius Caesar*

56   Kurt Weill (1900–1950)

57   *Our Man in Havana*

58   *Suor Angelica* (Sister Angelica)

59   *Maria Stuarda* (Mary Stuart)

60   *Martha*

61   Rosina. (We meet her as a young girl in *The Barber of Seville*).

62   *Lohengrin*

The Musical Theatre:
Operetta & Musicals

1 Who wrote the music to *My Fair Lady*?

2 Which Gilbert and Sullivan opera is subtitled 'Castle Adamant'?

3 Who wrote the music to *Les Misérables*?

4 When Lorenz Hart became ill, it was suggested to Richard Rodgers that he should work with Oscar Hammerstein II on a musical version of the play *Green Grow the Lilacs*? What was the resulting musical called?

5 Who was the Danish musical entertainer whose acts included *Phonetic Pronunciation*?

6 Who was the German-born tuba player, artist and entertainer who ran a series of festivals in the 1950s devoted to musical humour?

7 What was Gilbert and Sullivan's first, not very successful collaboration, produced at the Gaiety Theatre London on 23 December 1871?

8 Which operetta by Franz Lehar was first given in Vienna in 1923 with no great success under the title *The Yellow Jacket*, and later produced in Berlin to huge acclaim with Richard Tauber starring as a Chinese prince?

9 Who says, in a Gilbert and Sullivan opera: 'Ah, don't shrink from me, Captain. I'm unpleasant to look at and my name's agin me, but I ain't as bad as I seem'?

10 Who was Sullivan's collaborator in *Cox and Box*?

11 With whom did W. S. Gilbert collaborate in *Fallen Fairies*?

12 Which famous American composer of musical shows spent some time in London before the first world war, contributing numbers to West End musical comedies, and on 25 October 1910 married Eva Leale, daughter of the landlord of the Swan Hotel, Walton-on-Thames?

13 *Annie Get Your Gun* was composed by Irving Berlin. But the score was originally commissioned from another composer who died before he could start work on it. Who was he?

14 Gilbert and Sullivan again. Which high-ranking officer can: 'Hum a fugue of which he's heard the music's din afore, and whistle all the airs from that infernal nonsense Pinafore'?

15 Who was the Irish-born musician who went to America in the 1880s and got a job as a cellist before starting to compose a long string of operettas including *Babes in Toyland*, *Naughty Marietta*, *Sweethearts* and *Orange Blossom*?

16 Who, in a Gilbert and Sullivan opera, 'led his regiment from behind—he found it less exciting'?

17 The Spaniards have a form of operetta or musical comedy of their own which was at its peak in the 19th century. Placido Domingo's parents specialised in this type of entertainment and Domingo himself has sung a great deal of it. What is it called?

18 In Gilbert and Sullivan's ***Ruddigore***, Mad Margaret marries Sir Despard Murgatroyd. She becomes prim and proper, quite unlike her former self. But she is liable to lapses. She says to Despard: 'I sometimes think that if we could hit upon some word for you to use whenever I am about to relapse, some word that teems with inner meaning, it might recall me to my saner self.' What is that word?

19 What's the title of the musical based on the life of Edvard Grieg, first seen in New York in 1944 and in London in 1946?

20 Which operetta by Offenbach is about a pair of Swedish visitors to Paris?

21 At the end of *HMS Pinafore* Ralph Rackstraw gets to marry Josephine, the daughter of his former Captain. Who does the Captain marry?

22 Who collaborated with Richard Rodgers on *The Boys From Syracuse*, *Pal Joey* and *On Your Toes*?

23 In the mid 1920s Noel Coward heard a recording of *Die Fledermaus* and there and then made up his mind to write a musical show conjuring up the magic of old Vienna. It was a huge success in 1929. What was it?

24 In which Johann Strauss operetta does the 'Lagoon Waltz' occur?

25 Which Gilbert and Sullivan opera was premiered at the Fifth Avenue theatre in New York on 31 December 1879?

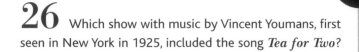

26 Which show with music by Vincent Youmans, first seen in New York in 1925, included the song *Tea for Two*?

27 *The King And I* was based on the novel *Anna And The King of Siam* by Margaret Landon. Who had the idea of turning it into a musical and played the Governess Anna Leonowens in the original New York production of the show in 1951?

28 Who was Andrew Lloyd Webber's collaborator in *Joseph And The Amazing Technicolor Dreamcoat*?

29 In a Gilbert and Sullivan opera, whose 'medievalism was born of a morbid love of admiration'?

30 Oscar Hammerstein II wrote the lyrics for 'Flower Drum Song'. Who wrote the music?

31 Split in Dalmatia was the birthplace of a successful operetta composer who spent much of his life in Vienna. He had three Christian names— Francesco Ezechiele Ermenegildo—and a double-barrelled surname half of which was Demelli. By what name is he known to the musical world?

32 Which great composer was the subject of a musical called *Lilac Time* which opened at the Lyric Theatre London on 22 December 1922 and ran for 626 performances?

33 The man who invented operetta in Paris was born Jacob Eberst. By what name do we know him?

34 When Offenbach's *La Périchole* was given its first performance in London it formed part of a double bill with a one-act piece by an English composer. What was it?

35 Who in a Gilbert and Sullivan opera tells the audience that he is an intellectual chap who thinks of things that would astonish you?

36 Mary Martin starred as a US Navy nurse in the initial run of *South Pacific*. What is her name and rank?

37 Who starred in the title role of Franz Lehar's *The Merry Widow* when it was first produced in London?

38 Who composed *The Desert Song*?

39 Who completed Sullivan's last theatre work *The Emerald Isle*?

40 Who is the leading male character in *The Merry Widow* who tells us all about his mis-spent youth at Maxim's?

41 On 28 April 1909 a highly successful show opened at the Shaftesbury Theatre in London and ran for 809 performances. In the first act an amateur aviator crash-lands his plane in a strange country where time has stood still. What is the name of the show?

42 Who is the eccentric prince who gives a party in Act II of *Die Fledermaus*?

43 Which show of 1927 brought a new seriousness to the musical theatre by touching on the colour question in America's Deep South?

44 Which Gilbert and Sullivan character says he is a thing of shreds and patches?

45 In which show by Ivor Novello do these songs appear: 'Fly home, little heart', 'Some Day my heart will awake' and 'Take Your Girl'?

46 Which show set in the 1920s opened at the Players Theatre in 1953 and later transferred to Wyndham's, where it ran for 2,074 performances?

47
What was the pen name of a composer whose real name was Jones, and whose stage works included *Tom Jones* and *A Princess of Kensington*?

48
In which light opera produced in 1902 does the character of Jill All-Alone appear?

49
In Leonard Bernstein's *West Side Story*, the young lovers are caught up in conflict between two rival gangs. One is the Jets. What is the name of the other, consisting of Puerto Rican youths?

50
Who in a Gilbert and Sullivan opera cannot escape from his indentures as an apprentice at the age of 21 because he was born on 29 February in a leap year, and so, reckoning by birthdays, is really only five?

1 Frederick Loewe (1901–1988)

2 *Princess Ida* (1883). Gilbert called it 'a respectful operatic perversion of Tennyson's poem The Princess'.

3 Claude-Michel Schönberg(1944–)

4 *Oklahoma*. First seen in New York in 1943.

5 Victor Borge (1909–2000). Variously described as 'The Great Dane', 'The Un-melancholy Dane' and 'The Clown Prince of Denmark'.

6 Gerard Hoffnung (1925–1959). ''The Bricklayer' was one of his memorable zany monologues.

7 *Thespis*, or The Gods Grown Old

8 *The Land of Smiles*

9 Dick Deadeye in *HMS Pinafore*

10 F. C. Burnand. This Triumveretta in One Act subtitled 'The Long Lost Brothers' was first staged in 1867.

11 Edward German (1862–1936)

12 Jerome Kern (1885–1945)

13 Jerome Kern

14 Major-General Stanley in *The Pirates of Penzance*

15 Victor Herbert (1859–1924)

16 The Duke of Plaza-Toro in *The Gondoliers*

17 Zarzuela. The word means 'bramble-bush' and recalls the 17th-century palace 'La Zarzuela', so called because it was built in an area of dense undergrowth.

18 Basingstoke

19 *Song of Norway*

20 *La Vie Parisienne*. The tourists are Baron and Baroness Gondremarck.

21 Little Buttercup

22 Lorenz Hart (1895–1943)

23 *Bitter Sweet*

24 *A Night in Venice*

25   *The Pirates of Penzance*

26   *No No Nanette*

27   Gertrude Lawrence (1898–1952)

28   Tim Rice (1944–)

29   Reginald Bunthorne in *Patience*

30   Richard Rodgers (1902–1979)

31   Franz von Suppe (1819–1895)

32   Franz Schubert (1797–1828)

33   Jacques Offenbach (1819–1880)

34   *Trial by Jury* by Gilbert and Sullivan. Royalty Theatre 1875.

35   Private Willis, on sentry duty in *Iolanthe*.

36   Ensign Nellie Forbush

37   Lily Elsie (1886–1962)

38   Sigmund Romberg (1887–1951)

39   Edward German

40   Count Danilo

41   The country was Arcadia. The show was *The Arcadians* with music by Lionel Monckton and Howard Talbot.

42   Prince Orlofsky

43   Show Boat (Jerome Kern)

44   Nanki-Poo as 'The Wandering Minstrel' in The Mikado.

45   *King's Rhapsody* (1949)

46   *The Boy Friend* (Sandy 'Wilson')

47   Edward German

48   *Merrie England*

49   The Sharks

50   Frederick in *The Pirates of Penzance*

Ballet & Dance

1 What is the name of the Prince in Tchaikovsky's ballet *Swan Lake?*

2 In the Prologue to *The Sleeping Beauty*, the wicked fairy says that if ever the infant princess pricks her finger, she will die. She does prick her finger at her 20th birthday party. What with?

3 A Spanish ballet with music by Manuel de Falla, scenery by Picasso and choreography by Leonide Massine who also created the central role of the Miller, was first seen in London in 1919. What is its name?

4 In 1938 the first performance was given in Brno of a ballet with music by Prokofiev based on a Shakespeare play. Which one?

5 In 1945 the first performance was given in the Boishoi Theatre of a ballet composed by Prokofiev, based on which fairytale?

6 Which southern Italian dance was wrongly said to be a cure for the bite of a spider?

7 In *Swan Lake* the ballerina has a dual role as the Swan Queen and the daughter of an evil magician who impersonates her. What are the two characters called?

8 What is the name of the princess who is presented with a rose by each of her four suitors on her 20th birthday?

9 Which ballerina born in St Petersburg in 1881 was world famous for her short ballet *The Dying Swan*?

10 Which of Tchaikovsky's ballets was first performed at the Maryinsky Theatre in January 1892?

11 Which ballet caused a riot at the Théâtre des Champs Elysées in Paris on 29 May 1913?

12 A theme in the last movement of Beethoven's *Eroica Symphony* also occurs in a ballet with music by Beethoven first performed in Vienna in 1801 about an important figure in Greek mythology. Which one?

13 Ponchielli's opera *La Gioconda* features a ballet sequence performed to which well-known piece of music?

14 When Verdi's *Aïda* was first performed in Lyons, a famous Egyptian ballet, the *Ballet Egyptien*, opened Act III. It was composed not by Verdi but by whom?

15 What was the name of the Russian impresario who in 1907 created a sensation in Paris with a production of *Boris Godounov* starring Feodor Chaliapin and went on to create a world-famous ballet company?

16 What was the stage name of the famous ballerina whose real name was Peggy Hookham?

Ballet & Dance

17 Which famous dancer choreographed Debussy's *Prélude à l'après-midi d'un Faune* for Diaghilev in Paris in 1912, causing a great scandal because it was thought too sexually explicit?

18 What was the name of the Royal Ballet before it assumed that name by royal charter in 1956?

19 Stravinsky's *Petrouchka* takes place during a Shrovetide Fair in which Russian city?

20 Who was the dancer, choreographer and ballet director who lived from 1805 to 1879 and was the virtual creator of the Royal Danish Ballet?

21 Whose music is used in *Les Sylphides*?

22 In which ballet does the ballerina go mad in Act I and become a Wili in Act II?

23 In 1951 the ballet *Pineapple Poll* was put on at Sadler's Wells Theatre. The choreographer was John Cranko and the music by Sullivan was arranged by whom?

24 In 1933 a ballet with songs called *The Seven Deadly Sins* was produced in Paris. Bertold Brecht wrote the words. Who wrote the music?

25 What is the name of the wicked fairy in *The Sleeping Beauty*?

26 Delibes composed a ballet subtitled 'The Girl With The Enamel Eyes'. What is its title?

27 Who was the choreographer of the film ballet *Tales of Beatrix Potter*, later adapted for the stage?

28 Who wrote the music to *Tales of Beatrix Potter*?

29 Who is the heroine of *Coppélia*?

Ballet & Dance

30 What is the name of the ship in *Pineapple Poll*?

31 Which Caribbean city gave its name to the Habanera?

32 Which ballet reopened in Covent Garden on 20 February 1946?

33 Which ballerina starred in the 1948 film *The Red Shoes*?

34 Who composed *Giselle*?

35 What is the national dance of Catalonia?

36 Which ballet with music by Maurice Ravel about the adventures of an Arcadian shepherd and shepherdess was first produced in Paris in 1912?

37 In which ballet does a pair of Bluebirds appear?

1   Siegfried

2   A spindle

3   *The Three-Cornered Hat* (or 'Le Tricorne')

4   *Romeo and Juliet*

5   *Cinderella*

6   Tarantella. Derived from the town of Taranto in Apulia, the 'heel of Italy', which also gave its name to the tarantula spider. Its bite is harmless even though the creature is large and threatening.

7   Odette and Odile

8   Aurora, in *The Sleeping Beauty*

9   Anna Pavlova (1881–1931)

10 *The Sleeping Beauty*

11 *The Rite of Spring* (Stravinsky)

12 Prometheus. He was a Titan sent to earth by Zeus to make men out of mud and water. He was sorry for them and stole fire from heaven to brighten their lives, an action which associates Prometheus with the idea of inspiration.

13 *The Dance of the Hours*

14 Alexandre Luigini (1850–1906) Part of the ballet music was appropriated by the music-hall performers Wilson, Keppel and Betty who devised a famous comic sand-dance to fit it.

15 Serge Diaghilev (1872–1929)

16 Dame Margot Fonteyn (1919–1991)

17 Vaslav Nijinsky (1889–1950)

18 Sadler's Wells ballet

19 St Petersburg

20 August Bournonville (1805–1879)

21 Frédéric Chopin (1810–1849)

22 *Giselle*

23 Sir Charles Mackerras (1925–)

24 Kurt Weill (1900–1950)

25 Carabosse

26 *Coppélia*

27 Sir Frederick Ashton (1904–1988)

28 John Lanchbery (1923–2003)

29 Swanilda

30 HMS Hot Cross Bun

31 Havana, Cuba

32 *The Sleeping Beauty*

33 Moira Shearer (1926–2006)

34 Adolphe Adam (1803–1856)

35 The Sardana

36 *Daphnis and Chloë*

37 *The Sleeping Beauty*

Incidental Music

1 Which Shakespeare play includes the song
'O Mistress Mine'?

2 Which great composer wrote incidental music for a
play called *The Ruins of Athens*?

3 Grieg's music for *Peer Gynt* is among his most popular
compositions. Who wrote the play?

4 Grieg's *Peer Gynt* music includes a dance for a
north African belly dancer. What is her name?

5 Grieg composed a beautiful song for the
faithful girlfriend who waits patiently for Peer Gynt's return
from his travels. Who is she?

6 In which Shakespeare play does the song
'It was a lover and his lass' occur?

7 Who composed music for a play entitled
Morning, Noon And Night In Vienna?

8 Franz Schubert wrote incidental music for a play about
a princess of Cyprus. Who is she?

9 Who wrote the incidental music for *Starlight Express*
(Kingsway Theatre, London 1915)?

10 Who wrote the lyrics for Andrew Lloyd Webber's
Starlight Express (Apollo, Victoria 1984)?

11 Which Shakespeare play includes the song
'Who is Sylvia'?

12 Who composed the music for James Elroy Flecker's
poetic play *Hassan* (His Majesty's Theatre 1923)?

13 Which two famous composers wrote incidental music for Maurice Maeterlinck's play *Pelléas et Mélisande*?

14 Roger Quilter wrote the music for a play which opened at the Savoy Theatre in 1911 and was revived annually for many years. Which play?

15 Who composed the music for a Greek production in Cambridge in 1909 of *The Wasps* of Aristophanes?

16 Shakespeare's *Henry VIII* includes a song about which legendary musician of Greek antiquity?

17 Who wrote the music for Henry Irving's production of *Henry VIII* at the Lyceum Theatre in 1892?

18 Who composed the incidental music for a production of *A Midsummer Night's Dream* at Potsdam in 1843?

19 Who wrote an overture and 15 items of incidental music for Byron's verse drama *Manfred*?

20 Henry Purcell's song *Nymphs and Shepherds* first appeared in which play by Thomas Shadwell in 1692?

21 Which British composer made his name with music for Shakespeare's *The Tempest* first heard in London at a Crystal Palace concert in 1862?

22 Which British composer wrote incidental music for the TV series *The Gathering Storm*, *Blackadder* and *Red Dwarf*?

23 Who wrote the incidental music for the tragic play *King Christian II*?

24 In 1809, Beethoven was asked to compose music for the play *Egmont*, including his famous overture with the same name. Who was the playwright?

1 *Twelfth Night*

2 Ludwig van Beethoven (1770–1827). For a production in 1811 of the play by August von Kotzebue.

3 Henrik Ibsen (1828–1906)

4 Anitra

5 Solveig

6 *As You Like It*

7 Franz von Suppé (1819–1895). The overture remains a popular favourite.

8 Rosamunde. The play, by Helmina von Chézy, staged in 1823, was a disaster.

9 Sir Edward Elgar (1857–1934)

10 Richard Stilgoe (1943–)

11 *Two Gentlemen Of Verona*

12 Frederick Delius (1862–1934)

13 Gabriel Fauré (1845–1924) for a London production in 1898; Jean Sibelius (1865–1957) for a Helsinki production in 1905.

14 *Where The Rainbow Ends*

15 Ralph Vaughan Williams (1872–1958)

16 Orpheus: Orpheus with his Lute

17 Edward German (1862–1936)

18 Felix Mendelssohn (1809–1847). The overture was composed earlier, in 1826.

19 Robert Schumann (1810–1856)

20 *The Libertine*

21 Sir Arthur Sullivan (1842–1900)

22 Howard Goodall (1958–)

23 Jean Sibelius

24 The German polymath Johann Wolfgang von Goethe (1749–1832)

Films, Radio & Television

1 Who wrote the *Warsaw Concerto* for the film *Dangerous Moonlight* (1941)?

2 Who appeared to play the *Warsaw Concerto* in *Dangerous Moonlight*?

3 Who composed the score of *Things To Come* (1936)?

4 In which film of 1945 was Rachmaninoff's second piano concerto used to create a romantic atmosphere?

5 Who was the bandit whose name forms the title of a Laurel and Hardy film of 1933 loosely based on an *opéra comique* by Auber?

6 Who wrote the music for the 1942 film *The First Of The Few* about the inventor of the Spitfire fighter?

7 Which Mahler symphony contains the theme from *Death In Venice* (1971)?

8 In 1948 John Mills starred as *Scott of the Antarctic*. Who wrote the music for the film?

9 Who wrote the music for Kenneth Branagh's *Henry V* (1989) and won an Oscar nomination for *Sense and Sensibility* (1995)?

10 What was the signature tune of *In Town Tonight*, the BBC programme which ran for 27 years from 1933?

11 What is the title of the signature tune to *Desert Island Discs*, first presented on BBC radio by Roy Plomley in 1942?

12 Which product was advertised on television to the tune of Bach's *Air On The G String*?

13 Which film music composer was the first musical director of *Saturday Night Live*?

14 Which prolific American film composer was born on 29 June 1911 and died on Christmas Eve 1975?

15 The children's TV programme *Blue Peter* has a very famous theme tune. What is its name?

16 Virtually every TV programme uses specific theme music; name the famous exception that uses only the ticking hand of an *Heuer* stopwatch.

17 The BBC Radio 4 programme *Just A Minute* uses a version of the *Minute Waltz* for its theme tune. Who composed this tune?

18 Which operatic music was chosen by British Airways for their TV advertisements?

1   Richard Addinsell (1904–1977)

2   The actor Anton Walbrook. The off-screen pianist was Louis Kentner.

3   Sir Arthur Bliss (1891–1975)

4   *Brief Encounter*

5   Fra Diavolo (Brother Devil). The opera and the film were loosely based on the career of a real life brigand, Michele Pezza, half priest and half villain who was hanged in Naples in 1806.

6   Sir William Walton (1902–1983)

7   No. 5

8   Ralph Vaughan Williams (1872–1958)

9   Patrick Doyle (1953–)

10   The Knightsbridge March from the *London Suite* of Eric Coates (1886–1957)

11   *By The Sleepy Lagoon* (Eric Coates)

12   Hamlet Cigars

13   Howard Shore (1946–)

14   Bernard Herrmann (1911–1975)

15   *Barnacle Bill*

16   *60 minutes*

17   Frédéric Chopin (1810–1849)

18   *The Flower Duet* from *Lakmé* by Léo Delibes (1836–1891)

Royal Connections

1 What is the British name for the tune known in the USA as *America*?

2 *Rule Britannia* was first performed at Cliveden in 1740 in a Masque with music by Thomas Arne. The Masque celebrated the early English king who is credited with founding the Royal Navy. Which king?

3 Which English monarch is credited with writing the part-song *Pastime With Good Company*?

4 Which character in Shakespeare makes a proposal of marriage and requests a reply in the following terms: 'Come, your answer in broken English; for thy voice is music and thy English broken.'?

5 Which monarch supplied the theme for Bach's sequence of 13 instrumental compositions known as *The Musical Offering*?

6 Handel wrote his *Water Music* for a river party on the Thames organised by which king?

7 For the coronation of which monarch did Handel write his coronation anthems?

8 Which king asked Handel to provide music for a grand firework display in Green Park, demanding as many martial instruments as possible—and no fiddles?

9 What's the nickname of Mozart's piano concerto No. 26 in D?

10 To whom did Mendelssohn dedicate his third ('Scottish') symphony?

11 Thomas Morley edited a collection of madrigals published in 1601 entitled *The Triumphs of Oriana*. Who was Oriana?

12 Elgar dedicated his *Nursery Suite* to two well-known little girls. Who were they?

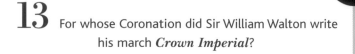

13 For whose Coronation did Sir William Walton write his march *Crown Imperial*?

14 *Land of Hope and Glory* formed the finale of a Coronation Ode composed by Elgar for the coronation of which monarch?

15 Which opera was written by Benjamin Britten for the coronation of Queen Elizabeth II?

16 Which march did William Walton write for the Queen's coronation in 1953?

17 Who is the rightful king of Barataria?

18 Which singer, pianist and composer wrote among other things *It's Only A Paper Moon*, *Nature Boy*, *Mona Lisa*, *Too Young* and *Ramblin' Rose*?

1	*The National Anthem: God Save the Queen*
2	King Alfred(c.849–899)
3	King Henry VIII
4	King Henry V (in conversation with the French princess Katharine)
5	Frederick the Great of Prussia. He played the flute.
6	King George I
7	King George II (in 1727)
8	King George II (in 1749)
9	The 'Coronation'. Mozart played the concerto in the presence of Emperor Leopold II in Frankfurt in October 1790.
10	Queen Victoria
11	Queen Elizabeth I
12	Princess Elizabeth and Princess Margaret, daughters of the then Duchess of York.
13	King George VI (in 1937)
14	King Edward VII (in 1902)
15	Gloriana
16	Orb and Sceptre
17	Luiz, drummer to the Duke of Plaza Toro in The Gondoliers (Gilbert and Sullivan).
18	Nat King Cole. His real name was Nathaniel Adams(1917–1965).

Orchestral & Chamber Music

1 What is the nickname of Haydn's *Symphony No. 94 In G*?

2 Camille Saint-Saëns was an important figure in the musical hierarchy of Paris and liked to be taken seriously. He composed his *Carnival Of The Animals* for a private occasion and refused to allow it to be performed publicly in his lifetime except for one number which he regarded as sufficiently serious. Which number?

3 In 1879 the *London Daily News* commented thus on a new composition:

'Mr Saint-Saëns has succeeded in producing effects of the most horrible, hideous and disgusting sort. Among the special instruments was a xylophone, the effect of which suggested the clattering of the bones of skeletons. A scarcely less hideous device was the tuning of the solo violin half a note lower than usual.'

What piece were they writing about?

4 Who wrote a symphony to celebrate the victory of the Duke of Wellington at the Battle of Vittoria in 1813?

Orchestral & Chamber Music

5
Who is the Danish composer whose fourth symphony is known as 'The Inextinguishable'?

6
Who composed the *Leningrad Symphony* in 1941 during the siege of that city by the Germans?

7
What is the nickname of Schubert's *Symphony No. 8 In B Minor*?

8
In 1899 Jean Sibelius composed the music for a patriotic pageant called *Finland Awakes*. A year later he arranged the final scene as an orchestral tone poem. What is it called?

9
Which instrument represents the swan in Sibelius's tone poem *The Swan Of Tuonela*?

10
What is the nickname of Mendelssohn's fourth symphony?

11
Which composition by Delius has a theme based on a Norwegian folk song?

12
Debussy's great orchestral portrait of the sea, *La Mer*, was completed in March 1905. That summer the composer took the proofs with him to correct during a holiday at a grand hotel on the English south coast. He described the town where he was staying as 'a little seaside town, silly as these places sometimes are. I will have to leave because there are too many draughts and too much music.' Which town was he staying in?

13
Which famous orchestral work with transatlantic associations was first performed at the Carnegie Hall in New York on 16 December 1893?

14
How many Pomp and Circumstance marches did Elgar write?

15
In which symphony did Beethoven first use trombones?

Orchestral & Chamber Music

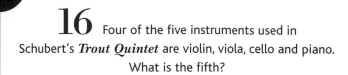

16 Four of the five instruments used in Schubert's ***Trout Quintet*** are violin, viola, cello and piano. What is the fifth?

10 Which composer wrote string quartets nicknamed 'The Frog', 'The Bird', 'The Razor' and 'The Sun'?

18 What number is the Haydn symphony known as the 'Clock'?

19 What is the nickname of Mozart's ***Symphony No. 35 In D***?

20 By what name do we know Mozart's ***Symphony No. 38 In D***?

21 What is the nickname of Schumann's ***Symphony No. 1 In B♭ Major***?

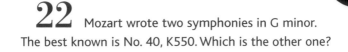

22 Mozart wrote two symphonies in G minor. The best known is No. 40, K550. Which is the other one?

23 By what name do we know Mahler's second symphony?

24 What is the name of the Swedish composer best known for his third *Swedish Rhapsody*, also known as 'Midsummer Vigil'?

25 Sibelius based several works on the national epic of Finland. What is its name?

26 Beethoven wrote his *Battle Symphony* for the Panharmonicon, a mechanical instrument invented by Johann Nepomuk Maelzel. The second movement of Beethoven's eighth symphony is said to have been inspired by another invention credited to Maelzel, designed to indicate time in music. What was it?

Orchestral & Chamber Music

27
Which American composer produced a work labelled 'Symphony 5½'?

28
Tchaikovsky spent some happy times in Italy and one musical result was the ***Capriccio Italien***.
He also wrote a string sextet entitled 'Souvenir de...' naming an Italian city. Which one?

29
Who wrote symphonies inspired by the sea, and the wastes of Antarctica?

30
What river which flows through Prague is the subject of a symphonic poem by Smetana?

31
Which Russian composer wrote a ***Spanish Caprice*** in 1887?

32 Which French composer visited Spain in 1882 and wrote a rhapsody named after that country which made his name?

33 How many symphonies did Haydn write for the London impresario Salomon?

34 What is the nickname of Beethoven's *Piano Trio In B♭ Op.97*?

35 Who wrote *The Symphony Of A Thousand*?

36 Mozart wrote three of a projected set of six string quartets for the King of Prussia, Frederick William II. They were designed to give prominence to the instrument the king himself played, without taxing him too much. What was his instrument?

1   *The Surprise*. So called on account of the sudden loud chord after the soothing start of the slow movement.

2   *Le Cygne* ('The Swan')

3   *Danse Macabre*

4   Ludwig van Beethoven (1770–1827)

5   Carl Nielsen (1865–1931)

6   Dmitri Shostakovich (1906–1975)

7   *The Unfinished*. Schubert only completed two movements of this work which then lay buried in a friend's cupboard for 40 years.

8   Finlandia

9   Cor Anglais

10   *The Italian*

11   *On Hearing The First Cuckoo In Spring*

12   Eastbourne

13   Dvořák's *New World Symphony*, No. 9 in E minor.

14   Five. He planned to write six.

15   *No. 5*. They appear to great effect in the last movement.

16   Double Bass

17   Joseph Haydn (1732–1809)

18   *No. 101* (in D major)

19   *The Haffner*

20   *The Prague*

21   *The Spring*

22   *No. 25*, K183

23   *The Resurrection*

24   Hugo Alfven (1872–1960)

25   *Kalevala*

26   The Metronome

27   Don Gillis (1912–1978)

28   Florence

29   Ralph Vaughan Williams (1872–1958)

30   Vltava (Moldau in German)

31   Rimsky-Korsakov (1844–1908)

32   Emmanuel Chabrier (1841–1894)

33   Twelve

34   *The Archduke*

35   Gustav Mahler (1860–1911). His eighth symphony.

36   The 'cello

Early & Baroque Music

1 What colour was Orlando Gibbons's swan?

2 *Clavicembalo* is the Italian word for which keyboard instrument?

3 Who was the Swiss musician and instrument maker who lived from 1858 to 1940 and made his home in Haslemere, Surrey where, in 1925, he started a music festival given by members of his family playing authentic old instruments or copies of them?

4 The sackbut (or, sometimes, shagbolt) is an early form of which modern instrument?

5 Who was the recorder player who, in 1967, formed the Early Music Consort and presented Radio 3's *Pied Piper* for six years?

6 If you wanted to perform on a racket would you blow it, bow it or bang it?

7 In which key is the first Prelude and Fugue in Bach's *48*?

8 What does the word 'baroque' literally mean?

9 Which Pope who reigned from 590 to 604 AD standardised the form of choral singing in church?

10 Why is the *viola da gamba* so called?

11 Which English 16th-century composer wrote a motet in 40 parts?

12 Which composer revived interest in the music of Johann Sebastian Bach by conducting his *St Matthew Passion* in Berlin in 1829?

13 Which Italian pioneer in the field of opera composed a famous *Vespers* for Mantua in 1610?

14 Which dance of French rustic origin became popular at court in the 17th century, occurred in many suites of the baroque period, and was adopted by many classical composers as the third movement of symphonies?

15 What is the name of the stringed instrument with a body like a halved pear and a fretted neck whose origins date back to 2000 BC, and which was widely popular in renaissance and baroque times?

16 *The Trumpet Voluntary* is an orchestral transcription by Sir Henry Wood of a keyboard piece by Jeremiah Clarke (1674–1707). What is its name?

17 Who was the harpsichordist born in Warsaw in 1877 who was interned in Germany in the first world war, lived in Paris in the twenties and thirties and had harpsichord concertos written for her by Falla and Poulenc?

18 Which suite for orchestra by Peter Warlock is based on French dances from Thoinot Arbeau's *Orchésographie* (1588–89)?

19 By what name do we know the first four of Vivaldi's set of 12 concertos Op.8 entitled *The Contest Between Harmony And Invention* ('Il Cimento dell'armonia e dell'inventione')?

20 Who was the first musician to hold the office of Master of the King's (or Queen's) Music?

1   Silver. 'The Silver Swan' is a much-loved madrigal by Gibbons

2   The Harpsichord

3   Arnold Dolmetsch (1858–1940)

4   The Trombone

5   David Munrow (1942–1976)

6   You would blow it. The Racket was an early form of bassoon.

7   C major

8   Bizarre. Some 18th-century writers used it as a term of abuse, signifying 'coarse' or 'old-fashioned'.

9   Gregory I (Gregory the Great). He is credited with promoting the development of a kind of plainsong which became known as Gregorian Chant.

10   Because it is held between the legs. 'Gamba' is Italian for 'leg'.

11   Thomas Tallis (c.1505–1585)

12   Felix Mendelssohn (1809–1847)

13   Claudio Monteverdi (1567–1643)

14   The Minuet

15   The Lute

16   *The Prince of Denmark's March*

17   Wanda Landowska (1879–1959)

18   *The Capriol Suite*

19   *The Four Seasons*

20   Nicholas Lanier. He was first appointed by Charles I in 1625 and resumed the office in 1660 under Charles II.

Church & Choral Music

1 Which hymn is normally sung to the tune *St Anne*?

2 Which oratorio did Mendelssohn compose for the Birmingham Festival of 1846?

3 What is the name of the popular choral work by the 20th-century composer Carl Orff which is based on secular poems by medieval monks and has an aria for a roasted swan?

4 In which city was Handel's *Messiah* first performed?

5 Which oratorio by Sir John Stainer written in 1887 went out of fashion for a time but is now often performed?

6 Who was the founder of the Glasgow Orpheus Choir and conducted it from 1906–1951?

7 Which contemporary English composer is a convert to the Greek Orthodox Church and has been much influenced in his music by his religious beliefs?

8 What collection of devotional music edited by Geoffrey Dearmer and Ralph Vaughan Williams appeared in 1906?

9 Who wrote the music to the Welsh national anthem, *Land Of My Fathers*?

10 Arthur Sullivan recorded in his diary that after a performance of his oratorio *The Golden Legend* at the Royal Albert Hall, an important person said to him: 'You ought to write a grand opera, you would do it so well.' Who was that important person?

11 What is the first chorus in Handel's *Messiah*?

12 Haydn's *Mass No. 9 In D Minor* composed in 1798 has a name which associates it with a British admiral. Which one?

13 Who was the boy soprano who in 1927 at the Temple Church under the direction of George Thalben-Ball recorded Mendelssohn's *Hear My Prayer*?

14 Who wrote the *Coffee Cantata* and the *Peasant Cantata*?

15 What oratorio by Sir William Walton caused a sensation at the Leeds Festival in 1931?

16 What hymn is normally sung to the tune *St Gertrude*?

17 What is the only duet in Handel's *Messiah*?

18 Who composed the *Chichester Psalms*?

19 Who composed the oratorio *A Child Of Our Time*?

20 The song *Nymphs And Shepherds* by Henry Purcell acquired new fame in the 20th century when it was recorded by a large choir of schoolchildren conducted by Sir Hamilton Harry. In which city?

21 For the centenary of which choral society in 1936 did Vaughan Williams compose his *Dona Nobis Pacem*?

22 For the opening of the Royal Albert Hall in 1871 Charles Gounod formed a large choir known as the Royal Albert Hall Choral Society. In 1888 it assumed the name by which we know it today. What is that name?

23 Who composed *A Mass Of Life* which was given its first complete performance in London in 1909 under the direction of Sir Thomas Beecham?

24 What is the work by Benjamin Britten which uses the Latin Mass interspersed with poems by Wilfred Owen?

25 Who completed Mozart's *Requiem*?

26 In church music, what word of Greek origin denotes a versicle or phrase sung by one choir or section of a choir in reply to another?

27 What Italian phrase is used to describe unaccompanied choral singing?

28 Which oratorio by Handel was written to celebrate the victory of the Duke of Cumberland at the battle of Culloden?

29 Stravinsky wrote an opera-oratorio with words by Jean Cocteau first produced in 1928 in a concert performance by Serge Diaghilev. It is named after a mythical Greek king. Which one?

30 Who is the patron saint of music?

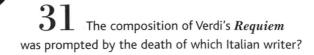

31 The composition of Verdi's *Requiem* was prompted by the death of which Italian writer?

32 *The Creation*, composed by Haydn, had its first public performance in which European city?

33 Which English choral composer, noted for his *Requiem*, celebrated his 60th birthday in 2005?

34 Name the French composer who wrote the *Requiem Op.5 (Grande Messe des Morts)*, known for its impressive orchestration of woodwind and brass instruments, including four antiphonal brass ensembles to be placed at the corners of the concert hall.

35 Which form of monophonic, unaccompanied singing, developed in the Catholic Church takes its name from Pope St. Gregory the Great?

36 Who composed the *Christmas Oratorio*?

37 In what year was the *Requiem in D minor*, composed by Gabriel Fauré, first performed?

38 Charles Gounod was best known for his opera *Faust*, but how many oratorios did he compose?

39 Elgar composed an oratorio in 1900, set to text from a poem by Cardinal Newman. What was the name of the oratorio?

40 By what name is Beethoven's *Mass in D major, Op.123* generally known?

1   O God Our Help In Ages Past

2   *Elijah*

3   *Carmina Burana*

4   Dublin (in April 1742)

5   *The Crucifixion*

6   Sir Hugh Roberton (1874–1952)

7   Sir John Tavener (1944-)

8   The English Hymnal

9   James James, son of Evan James who wrote the words. First performed in the Methodist Chapel, Maesteg, in 1856. Published 1860 in John Owen's *Gems of Welsh Melody*.

10   Queen Victoria (1819–1901)

11   And the Glory of the Lord

12   Lord Nelson (1758–1805)

13   Ernest Lough (1911–2000)

14   Johann Sebastian Bach (1685–1750)

15   *Belshazzar's Feast*

16   Onward Christian Soldiers. Sullivan named the tune after the wife of a friend.

17   O death, where is thy sting? Sung by alto and tenor.

18   Leonard Bernstein (1918–1990)

19   Sir Michael Tippett (1905–1998)

20   Manchester (in 1929)

21 Huddersfield Choral Society

22 Royal Choral Society

23 Frederick Delius (1862–1934)

24 *War Requiem*

25 Franz Xaver Süssmayr (1766–1803)

26 Antiphon

27 A Capella

28 *Judas Maccabeus*. This includes 'See The Conquering Hero Comes'. One hopes that Handel did not know of the brutality which earned the Duke the title 'Butcher Cumberland'.

29 *Oedipus*. The work, in Latin, is Oedipus Rex.

30 St Cecilia, martyred c.176 AD.

31 Alessandro Manzoni (1785–1873)

32 Vienna, 19 March 1799

33 John Rutter (1945-)

34 Hector Berlioz (1803–1869)

35 Gregorian Chant, plainchant or plainsong.

36 Johann Sebastian Bach

37 1888

38 Six

39 *The Dream of Gerontius*

40 *Missa Solemnis*

Light Music, Jazz & Ragtime

1 Which bandleader commissioned George Gershwin's *Rhapsody In Blue* and gave the first performance in New York's Aeolian Hall in 1924 with the composer as soloist?

2 Billy Mayerl was a brilliant pianist and composer of many short piano pieces. The best known of these published in 1917 has the name of a flower. Which one?

3 Louis Armstrong's nickname was Satchmo. What was it short for?

4 Ernest Bucalossi is most famous for a salon piece named after an insect. Which insect?

5 *In A Monastery Garden* and *In A Persian Market* are two of the best-known compositions of which composer of light music?

6 In 1888 Edward Elgar wrote the most famous of his salon pieces. Originally it had a German title—*Liebesgrüss*—but Elgar's publisher thought French would be more appealing. By what title do we know the piece?

7 In 1918 George Gershwin had his first big hit with a song that was taken up by Al Jolson. What was the song?

8 In the 1830s a 19-mile railway was built between St Petersburg and Pavlovsk, where an entertainment complex grew up rather like London's Vauxhall Gardens—indeed it was called Vauxhall. Beginning in 1856, a well-known conductor and composer of light music took his orchestra there for ten successive summers and later on for two more. Who was he?

9 Which musician, director of music at Copenhagen's Tivoli Gardens for 30 years and composer of the *Champagne Polka*, is known as the Danish Johann Strauss?

10 What instrument is associated with Django Reinhardt?

11 Who composed *Fig Leaf Rag*?

12 Which American composer of Swedish descent composed *Sleigh Ride*, *The Typewriter*, and *Plink Plank Plunk*?

13 Who composed the *Skaters' Waltz*?

14 What instrument did Jelly Roll Morton play?

15 Which Russian composer, at the request of conductor Nicolai Malko, made an orchestral arrangement of *Tea For Two* (Vincent Youmans) in less than an hour?

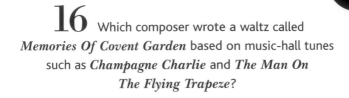

16 Which composer wrote a waltz called *Memories Of Covent Garden* based on music-hall tunes such as *Champagne Charlie* and *The Man On The Flying Trapeze*?

17 Which French jazz violinist partnered Yehudi Menuhin in a series of concerts and recordings in the 1970s?

18 In 1867 Johann Strauss wrote a choral waltz for the Vienna Men's Chorus. What was it?

19 Which British composer of light music played viola in Henry Wood's Queen's Hall Orchestra?

20 Which waltz by Johann Strauss might you read at breakfast time?

21 What was Irving Berlin's first big song hit in 1911?

22 Which American town was home to the Grand Ole Opry radio show first broadcast in 1927?

23 Which Berlin composer included the Glow-Worm Idyll in his 1902 operetta *Lysistrata*?

24 Who wrote *The Watermill* and *Elizabethan Serenade*?

25 Who was the star of the first sound film, *The Jazz Singer*?

26 Which pianist and musical scholar revived interest in the rags of Scott Joplin in the 1970s?

27 Which jazz musician is husband to Dame Cleo Laine?

28 Who is the composer of *Journey Into Melody*, *Jumping Bean*, *Portrait Of A Flirt* and *Peanut Polka*?

29 Who was the locksmith turned zither player who found fame and fortune via the soundtrack of Carol Reed's film *The Third Man* and was able to buy a tavern in Grinzing on the proceeds?

30 Which American entertainer gave us *The Prune Song*?

31 Which classically-trained cellist collaborated with the jazz violinist Stéphane Grappelli on the album *Anything Goes*?

32 The legendary jazz singer Ella Fitzgerald was born on 25 April 1917, in which American town?

33 The jazz musician Charles Mingus was famous for playing which instrument?

34 What word describes the characteristic way in which ragtime music places rhythmic accents on the weak beats?

35 Which jazz pianist composed the song *Honeysuckle Rose*?

36 Scott Joplin was famous for writing piano rags, but what is the name of the ragtime opera he composed, which is still performed today?

37 Who did the composer John Williams once describe as 'one of the great American masters of light orchestral music'?

38 The American jazz pianist Eunice Kathleen Waymon, who trained at the Julliard School of Music, New York, was better known by which name?

39 Miles Davis was legendary for his trumpet playing ability, but what instrument had his mother wanted him to play?

40 Pianist Fats Waller died in 1943, aged 39, of which illness?

1   Paul Whiteman (1890–1967)

2   Marigold

3   Satchelmouth (slang for 'big mouth')

4   The Grasshopper. Piece was *The Grasshopper's Dance*.

5   Albert Ketelbey (1875–1959)

6   *Salut d'amour*

7   Swanee

8   Johann Strauss II (1825–1899)

9   Hans Christian Lumbye (1810–1874)

10   The guitar

11   Scott Joplin (1868–1917)

12   Leroy Anderson (1908–1975)

13   Emile Waldteufel (1837–1915)

14   The piano

15   Dmitri Shostakovich (1906–1975)

16   Johann Strauss II

17   Stephane Grappelli (1908–1997)

18   *The Blue Danube*

19   Eric Coates (1886–1957)

20   *Morning Papers*

21   *Alexander's Ragtime Band*. First performed in public by female baritone Emma Carus.

22   Nashville, Tennessee

23   Paul Lincke (1866–1946)

24   Ronald Binge (1910–1979)

25   Al Jolson (1886–1950)

26   Joshua Rifkin (1944-)

27   Sir John Dankworth (1927-)

28   Robert Farnon (1917-2005)

29   Anton Karas (1906–1985)

30   Frank Crumit (1889–1943)

31   Yo-Yo Ma (1955-)

32   Newport News, Virginia, USA

33   Double Bass

34   Syncopation

35   Fats Waller (1904–1943)

36   *Treemonisha*

37   Leroy Anderson (1908–1975)

38   Dr. Nina Simone (1933–2003)

39   The violin

40   Pneumonia, on board an eastbound train, close to Kansas City.

Strike Up The Band!

1 The composer of *Colonel Bogey* is known to the world as Kenneth Alford. What was his real name?

2 Who wrote the marches *Hands Across The Sea*, *The Wolverine* and *The Transit Of Venus*?

3 Who was the Austrian general who suppressed a revolt in Austrian occupied northern Italy in 1848 and whose achievement inspired a famous march by Johann Strauss I?

4 Which march by Sir Malcolm Arnold includes a foghorn effect?

5 Who was the great figure in the brass band world who was a champion cornet player when young and later formed a band consisting of the best available players called Men O'Brass?

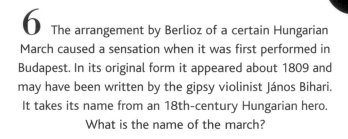

6 The arrangement by Berlioz of a certain Hungarian March caused a sensation when it was first performed in Budapest. In its original form it appeared about 1809 and may have been written by the gipsy violinist János Bihari. It takes its name from an 18th-century Hungarian hero. What is the name of the march?

7 What work for brass band, named after an English river, was composed by Elgar and dedicated to Bernard Shaw, who said 'this will secure my immortality when all my plays are dead and damned and forgotten'?

8 What is the home of the Royal Military School of Music?

9 Who invented the saxophone?

10 What instrument, made in 1898 for Sousa's band, encircles the player's body and terminates in a large bell which faces forward over the player's head?

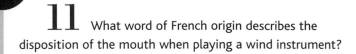

11 What word of French origin describes the disposition of the mouth when playing a wind instrument?

12 Which band, formed in 1855, was associated with a mill in the village of Queensbury, Yorkshire?

13 Which English composer wrote two suites for brass band (1909 and 1911) and later *A Moorside Suite* as a test piece for a brass band competition?

14 Who wrote the march *Cockleshell Heroes* intended for the film of that name? (1955)

15 What is the English nickname for the *Turkish Crescent*—an arrangement of small bells suspended from an inverted crescent fixed on a pole?

16 Who in 1923 composed the *English Folk Song Suite* for military band?

17 Which major brass band competition began at Belle Vue, Manchester in 1853?

18 From 1927, who was the conductor of the BBC Wireless Military Band?

19 Who was the American conductor and composer who, in 1869 in Boston, organised a massive Peace Jubilee with an orchestra of 1,000 and a chorus of 10,000 attended by Johann Strauss II.
He also composed *When Johnny Comes Marching Home*?

20 What is the tenor member of the tuba family whose name suggests (rightly) that it makes a pleasing sound?

1   Frederick Joseph Ricketts (1881–1945)

2   John Philip Sousa (1854–1932)

3   Count von Radetzky (1766–1858)

4   The Padstow Lifeboat

5   Harry Mortimer (1902–1992)

6   The Rákóczy March

7   The Severn Suite

8   Kneller Hall (since 1857)

9   Adolphe Sax (1814–1894)

10   The Sousaphone

11   Embouchure

12   Black Dyke Mills band

13   Gustav Holst (1874–1934)

14   Sir Vivian Dunn (1908–1995)

15   Jingling Johnny

16   Ralph Vaughan Williams (1872–1958)

17   The British Open Championships

18   B. Walton O'Donnell (1887–1939)

19   Patrick Gilmore (1829–1892)

20   The euphonium

Piano & Pianists

1 How many piano concertos did Rachmaninoff write?

2 Which great pianist married the daughter of Arturo Toscanini?

3 Who is the English pianist who was born in Saltash, Cornwall and made her debut at the age of 13 in 1929 in Harrogate playing Mendelssohn's *Concerto In G Minor*?

4 Who was the international pianist who in 1919 became Prime Minister of his native Poland and signed the Versailles Treaty on behalf of his country?

5 Who was the great pianist born in Poland in 1887, studied for a time with Paderewski, became famous above all for his Chopin, and continued playing in public until he was nearly 90?

6 By what nickname do we know Beethoven's *Piano Sonata No. 8 Op.13 In C Minor*?

7 Who was the Irish pianist and composer who settled in St Petersburg in 1803 and invented the term 'nocturne' to describe a dreamy piano piece?

8 Who was the first British pianist to win the Tchaikovsky Competition in Moscow in 1962?

9 Which British pianist won the Tchaikovsky Competition in 1970?

10 A certain 20th-century Canadian pianist had a great reputation as a Bach player; he was also notably eccentric and a brilliant mimic and entertainer. In 1964 he gave up the concert platform to concentrate entirely on recording. Who was he?

11 Who wrote *The Rustle of Spring*?

12 Who composed ten volumes of *Lyric Pieces* for the piano?

13 By what name do we know Beethoven's *Piano Sonata No. 23 Op.57 In F Minor*?

14 In which piano composition by Schumann do the characters of Harlequin, Florestan, Chopin and Paganini appear?

15 Who was the pianist who ran a famous series of concerts at the National Gallery in London during the second world war?

16 Which composer was successfully treated for depression by a hypnotist and thus enabled to complete his second piano concerto?

17 There was a Russian pianist who excelled at playing Chopin and was so renowned for the delicacy of his sound that someone dubbed him a *pianissimist*. He also had the habit of addressing his audiences from time to time with remarks mainly in praise of himself and to the detriment of other pianists. Who was he?

18 Who was the duo partner of Phyllis Sellick?

19 Which set of six piano pieces by Liszt could be considered prizes for the also-rans?

20 How many solo piano concertos did Camille Saint-Saëns compose?

21 Who was the composer of *Automne* ('Autumn')?

22 To whom was Beethoven saying farewell in his piano sonata *Les Adieux*?

23 What is the familiar name of Beethoven's *Piano Sonata In C♯ Minor Op.27 No. 2* ('Sonata quasi una fantasia')?

24 How many piano sonatas did Brahms write?

25 Who was the pianist who chaired BBC2's music quiz *Face The Music* (1966–1979)?

26 In his *Children's Corner Suite* Claude Debussy wrote a cakewalk for which doll?

27 Whose pictures include 'The Hut On Fowl's Legs' and the 'Ballet Of The Chickens In Their Shells'?

28 Who was the pianist who in the course of a long career (1925–1967) came to be regarded as the world's leading accompanist?

29 Who was the pianist and bandleader who wrote *Take The A Train*, *Mood Indigo* and a jazz version of Tchaikovsky's *Nutcracker Suite*?

30 Who was the Viennese pianist, composer and musicologist who wrote innumerable studies for the piano and dedicated his Complete Theoretical and Practical Pianoforte School (1839) to Queen Victoria, with whom he had played piano duets two years earlier?

31 Which Russian pianist had such large hands he could cover a thirteenth interval on the piano?

32 How many piano *concerti* did Mozart compose?

33 The word piano (used to describe an instrument) is a shortened form of which word?

34 Generally speaking, how many different sizes of modern-day grand piano are there?

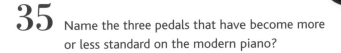

35 Name the three pedals that have become more or less standard on the modern piano?

36 How many *Gymnopédies* did Erik Satie write?

37 The book, and film adaptation of *The Pianist* tells the story of which Polish pianist?

38 The great pianist Franz Liszt was originally from which country?

39 Frédéric Chopin requested the Requiem of which composer to be sung at his funeral?

40 Which composer's *Third Symphony*, in C minor, requires an organist and two piano duettists?

1 Four

2 Vladimir Horowitz (1903–1989)

3 Dame Moura Lympany (1916–2005)

4 Ignacy Jan Paderewski (1860–1941)

5 Artur Rubinstein (1887–1982)

6 Pathétique

7 John Field (1782–1837)

8 John Ogdon (1937–1989) jointly with Vladimir Ashkenazy (1937–)

9 John Lill (1944–)

10 Glenn Gould (1932–1982)

11 Christian Sinding (1856–1941)

12 Edvard Grieg (1843–1907)

13 Appassionata

14 Carnaval

15 Dame Myra Hess (1890–1965)

16 Sergei Rachmaninoff (1873–1943)

17 Vladimir de Pachmann (1848-1933)

18 Cyril Smith (1909–1974)

19 Consolations

20 Five

21 Cécile Chaminade (1857–1944)

22 Archduke Rudolph (1858–1889)

23 Moonlight

24 Three

25 Joseph Cooper (1912–2001)

26 Golliwog

27 Modest Mussorgsky (1839–1881). In his *Pictures At An Exhibition*, written for piano, later orchestrated by Ravel

28 Gerald Moore (1899–1987)

29 Duke Ellington (1899–1974)

30 Carl Czerny (1791–1857)

31 Sergei Rachmaninoff

32 27

33 Pianoforte

34 Three: the 'concert grand', the 'boudoir grand' and the smallest—the 'baby grand'

35 Damper pedal (also known as the "sustaining pedal" or "loud pedal"), the soft pedal (or "una corda") and the sostenuto pedal (or "middle pedal").]

36 3

37 Wladyslaw Szpilman (1911–2000)

38 Hungary

39 Wolfgang Amadeus Mozart (1756–1791)

40 Camille Saint-Saëns (1835–1921)

Here & There

1 In the late 17th and early 18th century, fashionable concerts were held in the upstairs room of a coal merchant's house in Clerkenwell, London. Handel in his early London years was among those who took part. Who was the coal merchant?

2 In which year did the Henry Wood Proms begin?

3 Who was the young manager of the Queen's Hall who engaged Henry Wood to conduct the Proms?

4 Who was the first associate conductor of the Proms?

5 In which city would you find concerts accommodated in the Cloth Hall?

6 What is the name of the music, dance and drama school situated in the Lincoln Centre, New York that was founded in 1924?

7 What is the name of the hall which is home to Amsterdam's famous orchestra?

8 What is the American term for a crotchet?

9 In Indian music, what is the name of a sequence of notes arranged in a fixed ascending and descending order which may denote a certain mood or be associated with certain times of the day or of the year?

10 What was the name of English National Opera before 1974?

11 What is the term coined by the French musician Pierre Schaeffer in 1949 to signify music created from natural or man-made sounds other than those produced by accepted musical instruments?

12 Who was the founder and first director of the National Youth Orchestra of Great Britain?

13 What is the name of a type of orchestra found in south-east Asia, especially Indonesia, which largely consists of percussion instruments such as gongs, chimes and drums, but can include other instruments too?

14 Which orchestra in Austria is said to have been founded in 1842 by the conductor and composer Otto Nicolai?

15 Which open-air arena opened in 1919 near Los Angeles is the home of the Los Angeles Symphony Orchestra and stages many spectacular events?

16 Which estate near Lenox, Massachusetts is the setting for the important summer music festival founded in 1940 by Serge Koussevitsky?

17 Which Irish town has staged a festival devoted to unusual operas since 1951?

18 In which city is the Academy of St Cecilia?

19 What do the letters A.R.C.O. stand for?

20 Who was the English musicologist who started collecting English folk dances in 1899 and folk songs in 1905; and in 1911 founded the English Folk Dance Society?

21 Who founded the Tonic Sol-fa Association?

22 Who founded a school for gifted young musicians at Stoke D'Abernon in Surrey?

23 Who was the administrator of Covent Garden in the years just after the second world war?

24 Who was the Greek god of music and poetry?

25 Of the Nine Muses in Greek mythology which one was associated with choral dance and song?

1   Thomas Britton (1644–1714)

2   1895

3   Robert Newman (1858–1926)

4   Basil Cameron (1884–1975). He shared the conducting with Sir Henry Wood from 1940

5   Leipzig. The city's concert hall is the Gewandhaus (Cloth Hall)

6   The Juilliard School. The name is that of Augustus D. Juilliard (1836–1919) the cotton merchant whose generosity led to the school's foundation.

7   The Concertgebouw ('concert building')

8   Quarter-note

9   Raga

10   Sadler's Wells Opera

11   Musique Concrète

12   Dame Ruth Railton (1915–2001)

13   Gamelan

14   The Vienna Philharmonic Orchestra

15   The Hollywood Bowl

16   Tanglewood

17   Wexford

18   Rome

19   Associate of the Royal College of Organists

20   Cecil Sharp (1859–1924)

21   The Reverend John Curwen (1816–1880)

22   Yehudi Menuhin (1916–1999)

23   Sir David Webster (1903–1971)

24   Apollo

25   Terpsichore

Musical Quotations

1 Which Shakespeare play includes the following lines:

'This music crept by me on the waters
Allaying both their fury and my passion
With its sweet air' ?

2 Which Shakespeare play includes the line:

'I am never merry when I hear sweet music' ?

3 Which Shakespeare play includes the lines:

'Soft stillness and the night
Become the touches of sweet harmony' ?

4 Who said:

'There are two things that John and I do when
we're going to sit down and write a song.
First we sit down. Then we think about
writing a song' ?

5 Who wrote a song which has these lines:

'Play, orchestra, play
Play something light and sweet and gay' ?

---

6 Who wrote the lines:

'The harp that once through Tara's halls
The soul of music shed
Now hangs as mute on Tara's walls
As if that soul were dead' ?

---

7 Who said:

'Music is a method of employing the mind without the
labour of thinking it all' ?

---

8 Which Shakespeare character speaks the line:

'If music be the food of love, play on...' ?

---

9 Who said:

'Wagner's music is not as bad as it sounds' ?

10 Who wrote:

*'I like Wagner's music better than anybody's.
It is so loud that one can talk the whole time
without people hearing what one says'* ?

11 Who wrote:

*'Heard melodies are sweet, but those unheard
Are sweeter: therefore, ye soft pipes, play on;
Not to the sensual ear, but, more endeared,
Pipe to the spirit ditties of no tone'* ?

12 Who said:

*'Composers should write tunes that chauffeurs and
errand boys can whistle'* ?

13 Who wrote:

*'Hell is full of musical amateurs.
Music is the brandy of the damned'* ?

Round 18

14 Which Shakespeare play includes this thought:

'Take but degree away, untune that string,
And hark! What discord follows' ?

15 Who wrote:

'Musical people are so absurdly unreasonable. They
always want one to be perfectly dumb at the very
moment when one is longing to be absolutely deaf' ?

16 In 1886, Tchaikovsky wrote in his diary these thoughts about which famous composer:

'It annoys me that this self-inflated mediocrity
is hailed as a genius. (He) is chaotic and writes
absolutely dried-up stuff' ?

17 Who said:

'Music is a woman. She must be loved by the poet,
must surrender herself to him, in order that the new
art-work of the future may be born.
The begetter must be the artist' ?

Musical Quotations

18 Which conductor, who disapproved of women playing in orchestras, said:

'A pretty one will distract the other musicians and an ugly one will distract me' ?

19 Who is alleged to have said on his deathbed:

'Play Mozart in memory of me' ?

20 Who wrote:

'Beethoven can write music, thank God, but he can do nothing else on earth' ?

21 Who wrote:

'Oh my love is like a red, red rose That's newly sprung in June Oh my love is like a melody That's sweetly sung in tune' ?

22 Who wrote the lines:

'Whenever I feel afraid, I hold myself erect
And whistle a happy tune, so no one will suspect
I'm afraid' ?

---

23 Which character in
A Midsummer Night's Dream says:

'I have a tolerable ear in music; let's have the
tongs and bones' ?

---

24 Who said in reply to his critics:

'What you have said hurt me very much.
I cried all the way to the bank' ?

---

25 Who wrote:

'Music when soft voices die vibrates in the memory' ?

26 Who wrote:

'People are wrong when they say that opera isn't what it used to be. It is what it used to be. That's what's wrong with it' ?

27 Who wrote:

'There is sweet music here that softer falls Than petals from blown roses on the grass' ?

28 Who wrote in a musical journal in 1831 when Chopin appeared on the scene in Paris:

'Hats off, gentlemen, a genius!' ?

29 Who said about music:

'It is the only sensual pleasure without vice' ?

30 Who said:

'The English may not like music, but they absolutely love the noise it makes' ?

---

31 Who said:

'My music is best understood by children and animals' ?

---

32 Which composer said:

'If you develop an ear for sounds that are musical it is like developing an ego. You begin to refuse sounds that are not musical and that way cut yourself off from a good deal of experience' ?

---

33 Who said:

'Brass bands are all very well in their place – outdoors and several miles away' ?

---

34 Who said:

'I can't listen to that much Wagner.
I start getting the urge to conquer Poland' ?

35 Who wrote:

'[Tonality is] the art of combining tones in such
successions and such harmonies or successions of
harmonies, that the relation of all events to a
fundamental tone is made possible' ?

36 Who wrote:

'Muss es sein? Es muss sein! Es muss sein!
(Must it be? It must be! It must be!)' ?

37 Who once remarked:

'A musicologist is a man who can read music
but can't hear it'' ?

38 Who said:

*'I am not a fascist. I hate Tchaikovsky
and I will not conduct him. But if the audience
wants him, it can have him'* ?

39 Who said:

*'There's nothing remarkable about it.
All one has to do is hit the right keys at the right time
and the instrument plays itself'* ?

40 Who wrote:

*'Take Brahms: the product of the misty landscapes
of north Germany, his works are full of groping,
dreaminess and introspection. Mist gives a sense
of infinity; it may be only two feet deep but equally
it may cover the world, there is no knowing'* ?

1 *The Tempest*

2 *The Merchant of Venice*

3 *The Merchant of Venice*

4 Sir Paul McCartney (1942–) writing about his partnership with John Lennon

5 Sir Noel Coward (1899–1973). The song occurs in *Tonight At 8.30*, a collection of nine one-act plays in which Coward starred with Gertrude Lawrence in 1936. 'At the end of the first scene of *Shadow Play*,' recalled Coward, 'we belted out this song in the teeth of the audience while the stage staff were changing the scene behind us.'

6 Thomas Moore, Irish poet and musician (1779–1852)

7 Samuel Johnson (1709–1784)

8 Orsino (in *Twelfth Night*)

9 Mark Twain (Samuel Langhorne Clemens 1835–1910). 'Mark Twain' was a leadsman's call on Mississippi steamboats.

10 Oscar Wilde (1854–1900). In *The Picture of Dorian Gray*

11 John Keats (1795–1821) from *Ode on a Grecian Urn*

12 Sir Thomas Beecham (1879–1961)

13 George Bernard Shaw (1856–1950) from *Man and Superman*

14 *Troilus And Cressida*

15 Oscar Wilde. In *An Ideal Husband*

16 Johannes Brahms (1833–1897)

17 Richard Wagner (1813–1883) In *Opera And Drama* (1851)

18 Sir Thomas Beecham

19 Frédéric Chopin (1810–1849). Mozart's *Requiem* was performed in tribute to Chopin in the church of the Madeleine in Paris before a congregation of 3,000.

20 Ludwig van Beethoven (1770–1827) in a letter to Ferdinand Ries

21 Robert Burns (1759–1796)

22 Oscar Hammerstein II (1895–1960) *The King And I*

23 Bottom (when wearing the ass's head)

24 Wladziu Valentino Liberace (1919–1987)

25 Percy Bysshe Shelley (1792–1822)

26 Sir Noel Coward (1899–1973) in *Design For Living*

27 Alfred Lord Tennyson (1809–1892) from *The Lotus Eaters*

28 Robert Schumann (1810–1856)

29 Samuel Johnson (1709–1784)

30 Sir Thomas Beecham

31 Igor Stravinsky (1882–1971)

32 John Cage (1912–1992)

33 Sir Thomas Beecham

34 Woody Allen (1935–)

35 Arnold Schoenberg (1874–1951)

36 Ludwig van Beethoven, comment written on the finale of his *String Quartet in F Major, Op.135*

37 Sir Thomas Beecham

38 Pierre Boulez (1925–), quoted in Joan Peyser, *Boulez*, 1976

39 Johann Sebastian Bach (1685–1750)

40 Yehudi Menuhin (1916–1999), in *Unfinished Symphony* (1976)

Anagrams

1 REX AND ROBIN DO ALE (Russian composer)

2 RAID A DIVE (composer and one of his operas)

3 REASON I OCCUR (singer)

4 MERITING BETTER REPS
(composer and one of his operas)

5 DR AND REBEL ELF (pianist)

6 CENSOR RELIES ON LATINA
(composer and one of his operas)

7 COME SMALL GRANT (conductor)

8 BELIEVE IN THE FOOD
(composer and one of his operas)

9 GO DIDO COMPLAIN (singer)

10 FREUD LED AUSTRIAS MESS
(composer and an operetta he wrote)

11 VAST HOT SLUG (composer)

12 HAZY KEN IS MAD RIVAL (pianist)

13 RUDE SIDE FLICKER (composer)

14 ARCHER DRAWING (composer)

15 VULGAR THAMES (composer)

1 ALEXANDER BORODIN

2 VERDI: AÏDA

3 ENRICO CARUSO

4 BRITTEN: *PETER GRIMES*

5 ALFRED BRENDEL

6 ROSSINI: *LA CENERENTOLA*

7 MALCOLM SARGENT

8 BEETHOVEN: *FIDELIO*

9 PLACIDO DOMINGO

10 STRAUSS: *DIE FLEDERMAUS*

11 GUSTAV HOLST

12 VLADIMIR ASHKENAZY

13 FREDERICK DELIUS

14 RICHARD WAGNER

15 GUSTAV MAHLER

Tie-Breakers

Few people will know the right answers. Nearest guess wins!

1 Johann Sebastian Bach went to school in Eisenach. How many hours was he absent from school in 1695?

2 Jean Philippe Rameau wrote a number of harpsichord suites. How many?

3 Zdenek Fibich wrote a series of piano pieces entitled *Moods, Impressions and Reminiscences*. How many pieces are in the series?

4 Louis Moreau Gottschalk died in Brazil in 1869. In what year was he born?

5 The first theatre in Covent Garden was built by John Gay in 1732, 1747 or 1756. Which?

6 In what year did Khatchaturian compose his ballet *Spartacus*?

7 Schubert's works were catalogued by Otto Deutsch. How many D numbers are there?

8 How many piano concertos did Johann Christian Bach write?

9 How many violin concertos did Vivaldi write?

10 What metronome marking does Rachmaninoff give at the very beginning of his *Second Symphony*?

11 The largest piano built, the Fazioli F308, weighs how many kilograms?

12 The conductor Sir Thomas Beecham was knighted in which year?

1   103

2   56

3   376

4   1829

5   1732. John Gay died the same year.

6   1954

7   998

8   40

9   170

10 48

11 691(kg)

12 1916

Printed in China